Yoo-Hoo and
HANK WILLIAMS

GREGORY S. MOSS is a playwright and educator and currently serves as Head of the MFA Program in Dramatic Writing at the University of New Mexico. His plays include *Indian Summer, punkplay, Reunion, Billy Witch, House of Gold,* and *sixsixsix*. He has had his plays produced or developed at the Guthrie, South Coast Rep, and New York Theatre Workshop, among others. He is currently working on commissions from Playwrights Horizons and Woolly Mammoth as well as collaborating on a new musical based on the life and work of Hunter S. Thompson for La Jolla Playhouse. He divides his time between Albuquerque and Brooklyn.

@gregorysmoss
www.gregorysmoss.com

Yoo-Hoo and HANK WILLIAMS

A PLAY BY

Gregory S. Moss

OVERLOOK DUCKWORTH
New York · London

This edition first published in the United States and the United Kingdom in 2015 by Overlook Duckworth, Peter Mayer Publishers, Inc.

NEW YORK
141 Wooster Street
New York, NY 10012
www.overlookpress.com
For bulk and special sales, please contact sales@overlookny.com,
or write us at above address.

LONDON
30 Calvin Street
London E1 6NW
info@duckworth-publishers.co.uk
www.ducknet.co.uk
For bulk and special sales, please contact sales@duckworth-publishers.co.uk,
or write us at the above address.

Cataloging-in-Publication Data is available from the Library of Congress
A catalogue record for this book is available from the British Library

Book design and type formatting by Bernard Schleifer
Manufactured in the United States of America
ISBN 978-1-4683-1070-2 (US)
ISBN 978-0-7156-5017-2 (UK)
1 3 5 7 9 10 8 6 4 2

*My first play is dedicated to
its first cast: Hal, Holly,
Maureen, Nikole, and Paul*

Preface

I wrote most of this play in Nikole Beckwith's apartment, situated over a long-standing but not-so-hot pub, in Newburyport, Massachusetts, in the spring of 2002. Nikole's apartment looked like a chunk of the set pulled off of the sitcom *Friends* and planted in the middle of a quaint New England working class town. It had once been an office, and had the classic Yankee bare brick walls paired with cork-textured dropped ceilings that looked to be composed of some toxic material. Nikole's taste in décor merged 50s diner with 90s coffee shop—two styles she and I shared an enthusiasm for, both of which, in their ways, contributed to the setting of *Yoo-Hoo and Hank Williams.* Nikole's mom or dad had given her an iMac, already a few years old, and, when I got done with a day of substitute teaching across the river, I'd tromp over to her apartment and type away on that weird transparent Mac keyboard that seemed kind of cool just after the turn of the twenty-first century.

Of course the play I was writing was resolutely twentieth century —a kind of deliberate museum piece trying on a number of familiar tropes of American drama. It was my first real play, my first fully-realized multi-character play. Redolent of nostalgia for times and places I could only imagine, I think of *Yoo-Hoo* as a kind of reckoning, or at least paying cheeky fealty, to two of the dramatists who dominated mid-twentieth century American Modernism—Miller and Williams. Which makes sense, for a young person's first play: "Thanks Mom and Dad, I'm taking the car now, be back later."

Newburyport in the early 2000s was a happening place. I have a complicated relationship to my hometown (especially at that time— having retreated back there after a post-collegiate crash-and-burn in L.A.) but there's clearly something in the water, because the number of brilliantly talented artists who came of age there, at that time, defies mathematical probability. I don't just mean "small town talented" —not *Waiting For Guffman* talented—I mean people who have gone on to make significant contributions to the arts at a national level. The musician and visual artist Dylan Metrano; the charismatic singer/ songwriter/sometime actor Sam Buck Rosen; the Pelsue Brothers— Rory and Brendan—now working in New York City as playwright and director respectively; writer, filmmaker and dog-enthusiast Nikole Beckwith; Hal Fickett; Sean Baptiste—just to name a few. All these from a small seaside town of about 18,000, more valued for its quaintly preserved Yankee charm, than for any spirit of progressive or forward-thinking culture.

There was a great DIY spirit in the air in 2002, akin to what I imagined some fantasy version of New York City was like in the 70s, except without the drugs and poverty. Space was cheap and everyone was game. There was a constant flow of creative produc- tion in every medium and work that found new intersections between media as well. In various configurations, we all played in bands together, acted in each others' theatre pieces, put on dance shows and art shows, and generally made our own cultural fun. No one was watching us and there wasn't a strong need to put things online or to try to get rich 'n' famous, so we did everything we wanted to without fear of losing funding or reputation. There was no funding or reputa- tion to lose; just the warm shared language of friends making art with and for friends. It was the perfect circumstances under which to make art, and, as such, wasn't meant to last. Justifiable ambition and the need for bigger canvases broke up the family, which is good and natural, but that two or three year period was pretty golden, and served as a kind of pre-graduate training in (artistically speaking) figuring out what you want to do and *doing* it.

Yoo-Hoo and Hank Williams was a peak expression of that period, for me. Each project was meant to "get me in trouble"—that is, I wanted, with each new play, to push myself further away from my comfort zone. After a string of solo plays, I undertook to write my first "real" play, specifically building it from characters I knew my favorite local actors could play. If I had any idea what I was doing, it was from continued engagement with theatre from a very young age. I had little learned technique, but I'd acted in a lot of plays, directed a few, and read widely.

Despite the hazy, imagined southern setting of the play, it is a recognizable rendition of my hometown. Small towns, and the characters that inhabit them, still exert a fascination over me. I can't write about upscale characters in upscale apartments in fashionable neighborhoods in Manhattan or Brooklyn. Despite their popularity on American stages, that's not my terrain. I like eccentrics and hidden corners of the country. Regional specificity—of slang, cuisine, culture —seems to be dying a slow death by social media. The word "authen-ticity" is equally besieged, but I like it, and look for it, even if it's only provisional.

The play was first produced in the summer of '02, in a 50-seat theatre in a renovated leather factory downtown. I directed it, and cast my best friends, a former acting teacher and my mom in the play. I'd written it for them so that made perfect sense. I ran the light board and operated the CD player that comprised our sound sys-tem—not because I couldn't find anyone else to do it, but because I needed to do *something* while watching an audience watch my play. The performances were good—and, in small town terms, I would say it was a hit. We sold out most performances, extended an extra weekend, and closed before it got sad. We all made a little money. In the scrappy punk rock terms by which I measured my work, it was a success.

"Community" is a good word, but "community theatre" gets a bad rap. It implies vanity, silliness, a lack of rigor. I would counter that there are ways in which "community theatre" equals, and perhaps surpasses, art-making in the professional world. "Community theatre" can mean people making art to delight and engage the people closest to them. That's a good a use of time and energy, and as good a use of theatre, as any other. How many professionals strive to get to a point in their career where they can feel free of the self-consciousness and pressure that come from bigger budgets, limited space, and greater exposure? My friends and I started there, and this play is a product of that ethos.

As hard as it can be to reconnect with one's "early work"—like trying to collaborate with a precocious child actor who also happens to be *you*—I have enormous fondness for this play, and I am delighted to see *Yoo-Hoo* in print now, as a kind of document to the period of creative vitality and sense of community from which it grew.

Performance

Yoo Hoo and Hank Williams was first produced in 2002 by Independent Submarine Productions, Newburyport, MA. Directed by Gregory S. Moss.

YOO-HOO GIRL: Nikole Beckwith
THE PAPERBOY: Hal Fickett
AMY: Holly Little
THE SALESMAN: Paul Wann
BATTY: Maureen Daley

Lights and Sound: Sean Baptiste
Costumes: Bonnie-Jean Wilbur

Characters

THE YOO-HOO GIRL—mid 20s. Thin, awkward, painfully shy. Lives alone. Wears her father's old white button-down shirts and dungarees. Loves instant foods, movie star gossip magazines, stuffed animals, Hank Williams and Elvis.

THE PAPERBOY—teenager. Androgynous. Wears blue Dickies work pants, a green, white or maroon t-shirt, Keds. Earnest, damaged, shy.

AMY—late 20s. Pretty, big body and big smile, exuberant almost to the point of hysteria, loud, expressive. Former prom queen now lost. Overdresses.

THE SALESMAN—50-60. Cheap suit, suspenders, white short-sleeve button-down shirt. Gray, exhausted, charming. Always on the road. A very good salesman.

MADELEINE PRITCHARD aka BATTY—70-80. Insane. You can smell her coming—cat urine, cheap candy, and unwashed laundry. Legendary in this small town. Holds her deteriorating clothes together with safety pins and clothes pins. Saves everything. Lives in an enormous run-down house that all the school children say is haunted.

Setting

A sleepy, small town in an imaginary version of the American South, in an imaginary time in the early/mid-twentieth century. It is Spring when the play begins.

Prologue

THE YOO-HOO GIRL's *home.*

White spot on THE PAPERBOY *curled up on the floor stage right.*

The song "My Happiness" as performed by Elvis Presley begins to play.

Blue spot up stage left. THE YOO-HOO GIRL *steps into the blue light. Static slowly grows beneath the song, louder and louder until it overwhelms the music, crescendos, then dies abruptly with the lights.*

BLACKOUT.

Act One

1

Lights up on AMY *and* THE YOO-HOO GIRL *sitting on* THE YOO-HOO GIRL*'s porch in the sunshine.* AMY *has no shoes on. She is attempting to wind a doll-shaped music box with no results. She stares the doll in the face and shakes her.*

AMY

Rrrrr—sing! Sing!

(*Looks up. Pause. Smiles.*)

What a beautiful day! I love the Spring, don't you? It's like it all happens to me too, you know? Like I have little green-sprouts, buds coming up out of me . . . I get a very exciting feeling in my stomach. Like a tickling. Like going downhill fast on a bike. You know? It's a very specific feeling. . . . So what should we talk about? . . . Are you a—Scorpio?—No don't tell me a—Sagittarius!

YOO-HOO GIRL

Umm-hm.

AMY

You are? A Sagittarius?

YOO-HOO GIRL

Yes.

AMY

No way! I AM psychic! It's true you know I'm always getting these feelings, like I'll see somebody? On the street in front of Woolworth's or someplace and this voice in my head says, "He is cheating on his wife, look at the way he's got his tie all twisted up," or, uh, "Mmm-mmm, that lady is gonna slap those kids around when she gets home—it's in those creases around her mouth." I mean, it's not always bad things but always—something. Some like, information. Like a scent. I can smell it. It's just something I know.—I should have been a detective. I still could be. People trust me. They open up to me instinctively. Because, they know, that I do not judge. That's a very rare thing you know. They know they can just tell that I will accept whatever they have to say and smile and say something comforting.—If I were a detective, I'd be a good one 'cause I can get at everybody's secrets.

    (To music box.)

Except you.

YOO-HOO GIRL

I think she's busted.

AMY

You think?

YOO-HOO GIRL

Mmm-hm.

    (Beat.)

You wound her too tight.

    (Pause.)

But . . .

AMY

Hm?

YOO-HOO GIRL

How do you know??

AMY

How do I know . . .?

YOO-HOO GIRL

That what you smell—or whatever—that it's true? That you can trust it?

AMY

Well.—I was right about you wasn't I?

    (Pause.)

Wasn't I?

> *(Pause.)*

YOO-HOO GIRL

Ok.

> MADELEINE PRITCHARD (AKA BATTY) *with a white handker-*
> *chief in her mouth, her rotted clothes held together with*
> *safety pins, shuffles slowly in from stage left.*

AMY

Psst! Hey, look! It's Batty!

YOO-HOO GIRL

Where?

AMY

Don't look! She'll think we want her to come over here!

YOO-HOO GIRL

So?

AMY

So look at her! She's horrible! You wanna have a conversation with her? She's nuts! And she's mean! I heard she carries a brick in her purse to throw at little kids!

YOO-HOO GIRL

No way.

AMY

This is what I heard!

YOO-HOO GIRL

She's—

AMY

Ssshh!

> *(*AMY *puts her hand over* YOO-HOO GIRL*'s mouth to hush*
> *her.* BATTY *passes.)*

Phew! She's not interested in us—

> *(*AMY *removes her hand from* YOO-HOO GIRL*'s face and they*
> *relax.* BATTY *suddenly wheels around and faces them,*

pulling the handkerchief from her mouth and spraying saliva as she speaks.)

BATTY

Awhhh! Ah-HA! Ah-HA Ah-HA Ah HA! I know, I know! Oooh there ought to be a CURFEW for you people! Mhh! All you should be LOCKED INSIDE! In your stupid houses at 6:30 PM every night! You ought to be kept off the streets . . . you . . . you ought to be CRUCIFIED!

(BATTY begins to weep.)

(She dabs her eyes with her handkerchief.)

. . . You shits . . . you shits . . .

BATTY *exits crying, stuffing her handkerchief back in her mouth.*

AMY

Ughh! She sprayed me! I wanted the news not the weather!

YOO-HOO GIRL

She's a strange old gal.

AMY

She's disgusting! She's like an evil old witch!

YOO-HOO GIRL

You know what's scary? Someday you and me are gonna be like that too.

AMY

Like that?

YOO-HOO GIRL

Yup. Old and crazy.

AMY

We will?

YOO-HOO GIRL

Yeah. Of course. Won't we?

(Pause.)

By the way . . .

                    AMY

Yeah?

                    YOO-HOO GIRL

Amy?

                    AMY

Yeah?

        (Beat.)

                    YOO-HOO GIRL

I'm an Aries.

     YOO-HOO GIRL *smiles. Tableau.*

2

Later, nearby. THE SALESMAN *standing center stage with a pair of binoculars, a note pad, a pencil. He is looking intently through the binoculars. He pauses to scribble on his note pad. Again.* THE PAPERBOY *enters stage left. He stops, watches* THE SALESMAN.

THE SALESMAN *(Speaking to himself.)*

Bright yellow walls. Wooden cabinets. Out-of-date, dirty. Rice-a-roni, Kraft Dinner, a few cans of Campbell's Soup. Instant foods. Birdseye frozen peas, TV dinners, Salisbury steak and corn with—

THE SALESMAN *looks up and realizes he is being watched.* THE PAPERBOY *and* THE SALESMAN *regard each other a long moment.*

(Pause.)

THE SALESMAN

Fuck off kid.

(Pause.)

3

THE PAPERBOY *and* YOO-HOO GIRL, *seated on the couch, going through a shoe box full of old photos.* YOO-HOO GIRL *is looking intently at the pictures.* THE PAPERBOY *is mostly looking at her.*

YOO-HOO GIRL

Who's that?

THE PAPERBOY

Uh—my aunt Carrie. And her dog.

YOO-HOO GIRL

This one?

THE PAPERBOY

I don't know.

(YOO-HOO GIRL *holds up another snapshot.*)

My cousin Andy. He used to ride me around on this bike he had. He rode me on the handlebars when we used to visit him and my aunt in the summer. This one time, we were just riding around, they live up north a little, lots of hills and we were just burning down this one hill, and Andy's laughing, I'm laughing, we're going really fast, and he's got his head down and all of the sudden Andy turns his head back to me, there's a sick kind of light in his eyes, he says, "You know my brakes don't work, right?"—

YOO-HOO GIRL

—No!—

THE PAPERBOY

—And so I start screaming, and squirming and Andy's fighting me to keep still—like, *hugging* me to him, holding me in place, so he can steer and stuff and I'm screaming for him to LET ME OFF but still he's got me—and then there's this intersection below, at the bottom of the hill, the light turning green so the traffic's flowing, flowing across, against us, and we. Can't. Stop. We're falling down this hill, I'm screaming to the cars down there "Stop! Stop! Please! We've got no brakes! Please! Stop!"

YOO-HOO GIRL

And—

THE PAPERBOY

And—

YOO-HOO GIRL

What happened?

THE PAPERBOY

I—don't know, it's a blur kind of, like—there was some honking and I think the light changed. Something happened. I guess I closed my eyes.

(Pause.)

We rode the rest of the way to the corner store and had cokes and played pinball.

(Pause.)

He did a lot of weird things. He didn't have any friends. He used to keep live bugs in his pockets. He would take them out to give to the girls he liked at school. Then—I guess one day he goes up to this big graveyard on a hill after school out by where he lives. He takes off all his clothes and starts running around jumping and biting at the air. Like a dog. Someone called the police, and when they asked him he told the cops he was trying to catch birds in his mouth.

(Pause.)

Got put away. That's what my mom told me.

(Pause.)

Maybe he had brakes. Maybe he just wanted to scare me. To scare us both.

(Pause.)

He was really good at pinball, though.

(Pause.)

YOO-HOO GIRL

Who's this?

THE PAPERBOY

That? Those are my parents! Before I was born. Looks like my mom's pregnant, though.

YOO-HOO GIRL

These are your parents?—I hate them.

THE PAPERBOY

Why? They're just dumb hicks!

YOO-HOO GIRL

I hate them.

THE PAPERBOY

Why? You don't even know them.

YOO-HOO GIRL

'Cause they're so happy. And cute. This is the cutest goddamn picture I've ever seen! They've got everything they want, your mom smilin' in her dress and pregnant—they've got everything they want and they're stuck in there! I wanna get stuck! I wanna get stuck! I wanna fall in love and get stuck in a picture and never move again.

THE PAPERBOY

—they broke up—

YOO-HOO GIRL

Not in the picture, they didn't. In that picture, they are *in*-love, *for*-ever.

Pause. YOO-HOO GIRL *stares at the picture.* THE PAPERBOY *stares at her.*

THE PAPERBOY

There was some guy looking in your window before.

YOO-HOO GIRL

Huh?

THE PAPERBOY

Some guy with a notebook. When I came in. He was looking in at you.

YOO-HOO GIRL

. . . What was he doing?

THE PAPERBOY

I don't know. Taking notes. Watching you.

YOO-HOO GIRL

Out there? From the window?

(She stands and goes to the window.)

No one out there now.

THE PAPERBOY

He was across the street. I saw him when I was walking up the street. He looked at me.

YOO-HOO GIRL

—That's ok I guess. I wasn't up to much today anyway. Probably got bored.

THE PAPERBOY

I don't know. He was kinda—

YOO-HOO GIRL

What'd he look like?

THE PAPERBOY

He said something.

YOO-HOO GIRL

What?

THE PAPERBOY

He said something to me.

YOO-HOO GIRL

Did he?

THE PAPERBOY

Yes. Something rude.

YOO-HOO GIRL

What was it?

THE PAPERBOY

You don't wanna know.

YOO-HOO GIRL

What'd he say?

THE PAPERBOY

He told me to—"fuck off."

YOO-HOO GIRL

He did?

THE PAPERBOY

Yes.

YOO-HOO GIRL

That is rude.

THE PAPERBOY

Yeah.

YOO-HOO GIRL

For no good reason?

THE PAPERBOY

'Cause I saw him. I think. 'Cause I caught him looking at you.

    (Beat.)

YOO-HOO GIRL

Well, he's out there and we're in here. And I got you to protect me, right?

    (Pause.)

THE PAPERBOY

So. I gotta go finish my route now. You can. Hold on to those pictures for a while. If you want.

YOO-HOO GIRL

I'd like that.

THE PAPERBOY

Like for a couple of days more, if you want to, or I can come back for 'em.

YOO-HOO GIRL

That's very nice.

THE PAPERBOY

I could come back for them tomorrow, if—

YOO-HOO GIRL

Yes. Ok. Tomorrow.

(*Beat.*)

That's very sweet of you.

THE PAPERBOY

Yeah. Ok. Yeah.

(*Beat.*)

Yeah.

THE PAPERBOY *exits.* YOO-HOO GIRL *turns back to the photographs.*

4

A distorted voice, that of THE SALESMAN, *heard on a tape as the lights slowly come up. We see the* YOO-HOO GIRL *in her home cleaning and arranging things.* YOO-HOO GIRL *puts on a Hank Williams record ("Settin' the Woods On Fire") and exits. Returns, dancing, with a white mixing bowl. She is making chocolate pudding.* YOO-HOO GIRL *sings off-key with the song. She sits center stage on the couch. Mixing and singing.*

THE SALESMAN (V.O.)

Bright yellow walls. Wooden cabinets. Out-of-date, dirty. Rice-A-Roni, Kraft Dinner, a few cans of Campbell's Soup. Instant foods. Birds Eye frozen peas, TV dinners, Salisbury steak and corn with mashed potatoes and an apple cobbler dessert. Jell-O mix in cherry and lime. Tapioca pudding and whipped cream. Oscar Mayer hotdogs. Wonder bread. *True Confessions* magazines. Yoo-Hoo. Peter Pan peanut butter. *True Confessions. True Romance*—movie star magazines. *Casper the Friendly Ghost* comic books. Photo albums. Lots of them. Fake fruit in a glass bowl. Candy dish filled with peppermints. Rotten couch. Pink fuzzy slippers. Mmm. A record player, a child's record player, that suitcase kind. Brown. It's on all the time.

(Pause.)

Thin white curtains on the windows.

There is a knock at the door. Music fades. She freezes. Another knock. She looks at the door.

Another knock.

(Pause.)

5

BATTY*'s house. She stands in front of an easel, singing "The Teddy Bears' Picnic" quietly to herself and painting. She is painting with great care and concentration. Her body is blocking the canvas. There is a knock.* BATTY *goes to the door. As she walks away from the easel, we see her canvas is covered with a single shade of slate gray.* THE PAPERBOY *stands in the doorway with his sack.*

BATTY

Yes?

THE PAPERBOY

Yes, hi. I'm the paperboy.

BATTY

Yes, I can see you're the paperboy. What do you want?

THE PAPERBOY

I'm here to collect. It's Thursday.

BATTY

Collect what?

THE PAPERBOY

Money. For the newspaper.

BATTY

So you're the one that's been leaving those?

THE PAPERBOY

Yeah. That's my job. You told them you wanted me to.

BATTY

Oh did I?

THE PAPERBOY

You're on my list. Look—here—

>*(He pulls a small notebook out of his bag and shows.*
>BATTY *her name on the list.)*

See?

BATTY

>*(Genuinely surprised.)*

That's me!

THE PAPERBOY

Yes.

BATTY

So. I gotta pay for these?

THE PAPERBOY

Yes.

BATTY

But they were already here. Why do I gotta pay for something I already got?

>*(Pause.)*

You people are fucking nuts, you know that?

THE PAPERBOY

. . . Well . . .

>*(Pause.)*

BATTY

Come inside.

>THE PAPERBOY *enters.* BATTY *steps back to appraise him.*

BATTY

Hmmm . . . you're pretty.

>*(Coming closer, sniffing him.)*

Mmm . . . are you a little boy? Or a girl?

THE PAPERBOY

. . . I'm a boy.

BATTY

You are? Are you sure? 'Cause you're pretty like a girl! Pretty like a fat pig-tailed girl.

>*(Sniffs him.)*

You smell pretty!

THE PAPERBOY

Yeah.

>*(Pause.)*

So I have to collect four eighty-five.

BATTY

Four eighty-five?

THE PAPERBOY

Uh—

BATTY

Four dollars and eighty-five cents? Four dollars and—what do I look like Howard-fucking-Hughes? I'm a crazy old woman! You leeches! Four eighty-five! I don't know if I've even ever *seen* four dollars and eighty-five cents in the same place before! What's this news printed on, gold cloth and butterfly wings?

THE PAPERBOY

No, no—it's just, you know, *paper*, but—um—you haven't paid your bill for five weeks. It's normally only ninety-five cents a week but you—

BATTY

But—but how was I to know? No one told me I owed money. I thought those newspapers were presents!

THE PAPERBOY

Well—I left a note in the mailbox—

BATTY

I don't read those. I throw those away. Nothing that comes through the mail slot. I take everything that comes through the mail slot and put it in a box. I get boxes from out behind the Mister Grocer. They let me take 'em free! Big empty cardboard boxes from Tide and Joy and Kix. I have so many boxes! It makes me feel rich, y'know, like all that stuff was mine once. It was FULL once and I just USED IT UP! Heh! But I DO NOT look at the mail. I put it in the boxes and lock it in the basement. And now . . . you know what?

THE PAPERBOY

What??

BATTY

(Interrupting immediately.)

—I HAVE OVER ONE HUNNERD AND SIXTY-SEVEN BOXES!

BATTY *dances around, laughs and claps her hands in glee.*

THE PAPERBOY

Oh. Ah. "Wow." But . . .

(Pause.)

Why?

BATTY

Because when the nuclear war comes I'm gonna need something to read down there. All of you will be incinerated—fire blasting right through you—and your family will be eating your burnt up body, your skin—but me? I'll be down in my basement drinking lemonade and looking at the Sears catalogue from 1947! Until things cool off upstairs! Ha! Then I'll climb out and wait for God to come pick me up in his new transistor-driven chariot made out of pure sound waves and chrome! Hoo-hoo-hoo!

(Pause. BATTY *calms down.)*

Do you know? In nuclear war? It's not the *radiation* that kills you . . .

(Leaning in.)

It's the boredom.

(An idea occurring to her.)

I'll be right back . . .

> BATTY *exits.* THE PAPERBOY *stares at her canvas. She
> re-enters carrying two filthy Ball jars filled with pennies.*

BATTY

Uh! Ok! Here you are here you are! Eh? Even a tip in there for you—

(Looks at jars.)

—I think—Ok—come get it now.

> THE PAPERBOY *walks over to take the jars. As he does,*
> BATTY *grabs his wrist and pulls him in close.*

BATTY

Don't you wanna thank me?

THE PAPERBOY

Oh—"thanks."

BATTY

No! You kiss me now. Here.

*(*BATTY *points to her cheek.)*

You kiss me now. Go.

> *She closes her eyes.* THE PAPERBOY *hesitates, then leans
> in to kiss her cheek. She turns abruptly and gets his kiss
> on the lips.* THE PAPERBOY *shrinks back.*

BATTY

Ha! Ha! That's what I like! Heh! Are you sure you're a little boy? 'Cause
you kiss like a little girl does! So pretty—heh! Ok—now you leave.

(Pause.)

Get out of here!

> THE PAPERBOY *exits quickly.* BATTY *turns back to her paint-
> ing and begins to sing softly to herself.*

6

YOO-HOO GIRL'S *home.* THE SALESMAN *has spread an array of household products on the coffee table: soaps, lotions, detergents, etc. He sits on the couch. He notices the doll-shaped music box on the table. He picks her up, tips her upside down to look up her skirt. Nothing of interest. Puts her down.*

YOO-HOO GIRL *returns with two plastic bowls filled with garish snacks.*

YOO-HOO GIRL

Don't have much to offer you, I'm afraid. There's, some, peanuts in the kitchen, I think, but, they're probably pretty stale. You want me to go check?

THE SALESMAN

Aw, no, no this is swell. This is just swell.

YOO-HOO GIRL

I usually have more stuff around, but I.

(Beat.)

I guess wasn't expecting anybody.

THE SALESMAN

You do a lot of entertaining?

YOO-HOO GIRL

Just myself mostly.

THE SALESMAN

Ha! I'll bet, I'll bet. So ah—your parents coming home soon?

YOO-HOO GIRL

My *parents*? Oh. Oh no! Ha! No. I'm—I'm twenty-four years old! My parents! Oh man!

THE SALESMAN

You're twenty-four years old?

THE YOO-HOO GIRL *nods.*

THE SALESMAN

No!

THE YOO-HOO GIRL *nods.*

THE SALESMAN

No! You have such a young face.

YOO-HOO GIRL

Well.

(Pause.)

THE SALESMAN

This is quite a place you have here, little lady.

YOO-HOO GIRL

I did the decorating myself.

THE SALESMAN

Really? I might have guessed. I can see, just from looking at you, that *you, have, taste.*

YOO-HOO GIRL

Yes I do.

THE SALESMAN

Yes, you do. You're a big—music fan, I see.

YOO-HOO GIRL

I guess I am. Yeah. I'm, I'm pretty crazy about it! Actually. If I was born with any kind of voice or talent at all I'm sure I woulda been a singer. Not the star kind but y'know like one of those—whattaya call 'em— back up girls? Who dance in the back? I'd like that. I spend all my money on records. Usually I always got something playing. You want me to put something on?

THE SALESMAN

Aw, no, that's ok, not right now. I'm just talking here to you now. Trying to get to know you.

YOO-HOO GIRL

Not much to know.

THE SALESMAN

Oh. I don't think that's true.

(Pause.)

I sell Amway. That's why I'm here. I come to people's homes, knock on their doors, they let me in, I spread out my wares, cup of coffee, we chat, and then at *some* point I turn and I say—

YOO-HOO GIRL

You say—

THE SALESMAN

. . . "do any of these products strike your fancy, ma'am?" And then I smile.

(He smiles.)

Usually she'll pick out something. Something small—a tube of tooth-paste, a bar of soap . . . *nylons*—

(Beat.)

—then we shake hands, I pack up, and it's off to the next house. That's usually how it works.

YOO-HOO GIRL

Usually.

THE SALESMAN

But—hey, but look— You seem like a decent girl. I'm gonna be candid with you. I'm gonna cut out all of the uh pardon-my-French *horseshit* I usually shovel, and we are gonna just *talk*, you and me. We are just two people, two individuals, brought together by circumstance, talking, getting to know one another a little better. That alright?

YOO-HOO GIRL

Yes.

THE SALESMAN

It's alright with you?

YOO-HOO GIRL

Yes. Yes.

THE SALESMAN

Well alright then.

(Pause.)

I believe in these products. Of course I do. I believe in them. And I could name a thousand other jobs that I would be qualified—over-qualified, believe me, to do. I have had many professions so many *careers* in my life—done things that've taken me back and forth across the country and met all *kinds* of crazy people along the way—but my real calling, the thing that fulfills me, the thing that gets me up out of bed in the morning and leaves me smiling and content when I lay myself down to sleep at night—do you know what that is?

YOO-HOO GIRL

No.

THE SALESMAN

No? Well, I'll tell you: It's being here with you.

YOO-HOO GIRL

No.

THE SALESMAN

Oh yes. You see? Being here with you. With this case full of *soaps* and *lotions* and whatever else, and these *products*, as good as they are, as much as I believe in them they're just props. They are just an excuse.

YOO-HOO GIRL

An excuse.

THE SALESMAN

An excuse, for people, for us, to be together.

(Picks up a bar of soap.)

This. Hm? This. What is this?

YOO-HOO GIRL

Soap.

THE SALESMAN

It *is* soap. But. It's not *just* soap. It's not just soap. This, is the means we use to connect. You see? Take this. Take it. Come on.

(She does, awkwardly pinching one end of the soap as THE SALESMAN *holds the other.)*

There. See? Now: we are connected. You and me. It's a bridge.

(Pause as they stare at each other, each holding one end of the bar of soap.)

You need this, don't you? You do.

YOO-HOO GIRL

I do.

THE SALESMAN

What?

YOO-HOO GIRL

Yes. I do.

THE SALESMAN

Of course you do. We *all* do. I could see that about you. Your eyes, they have a hungry cast. A lonely look. It's ok. There's no shame in that. You live alone—

YOO-HOO GIRL
(Interrupting with quiet urgency.)

Hand me something else.

THE SALESMAN

Well, ok. Ok. Now here's—

(Pulls out a tube of toothpaste.)

This. Right? What is it? What does it mean? By itself: nothing. And people seem so far away from each other, don't they? Stranded on these little islands, signaling to each other, reaching but never really—

(Gestures with toothpaste.)

And now—We are together. This way we feel less alone.

YOO-HOO GIRL

Umm-hm.

THE SALESMAN

It is better. It is better this way, I think.

> *(Pause.)*

So.

> *(Beat.)*

"Do any of these products strike your fancy, ma'am?"

> *(*THE SALESMAN *laughs and shakes his head. Pause.)*

I look at you sitting there with your feet tucked up and that look in your eyes. You know what I'm thinking? "I'm gonna eat you." When I look at you there. I sincerely feel that. I am going to devour you.

YOO-HOO GIRL

You are?

THE SALESMAN

Yes. I am.

> *(Pause.)*

What do you think of that?

> *They stare at each other. Pause. Music: "Someday You'll Want Me To Want You" by Patsy Cline.*

7

AMY *alone in her house. She is on her hands and knees trying to coax her cat out from under the couch.*

AMY

Huey? Huey? Huey for God's sake! Huey come here. Huey, I just—I just want to talk to you, Huey. Come here. Huey, will you please come out from under there and just come over here and talk to me, you stupid cat?

(Sighs. Sits.)

Coo-coo? Meow-meow? Kiss-kiss?

(Pause.)

You peed on my favorite skirt and I didn't even get mad, Huey! I am so good to you! I'm like your best friend, Huey, in the world! You don't even have anyone but me!—But you know what? I don't even want you, Huey. I don't. My mother made me take you when she got her new couch. I never wanted you. I don't want a cat!

(Pause.)

I do want a cat. But I want a different cat, Huey. I want a cat that's gonna play with me and sit on my lap. That's your job, Huey.—I want a cat that's gonna take me out for picnics by the river and dinner at fancy restaurants and who'll pay for me at the movies and hold the door to let me in. I want a cat that's handsome and tall with big hands and black hair and a black leather jacket and looks like Robert Mitchum but talks like Marlon Brando and who'll walk through the door and make my mom have a fatal HEART ATTACK! I wanna run through the house screaming and knocking everything down—tear the plastic covers off the furniture! And jump in your convertible and take off across Texas and Arizona and drive all night every night non-stop with the top down and the hot desert wind coming through our hair and me and you we just FUCK like crazy rabbits without stopping! We don't even pull over, just keep going, me on your lap, your foot on the accelerator, the roads empty and the car going faster and faster and the moon above smiling and nodding, cheering us on, telling us "Hell, Yes!"

(Pause.)

That's the kind of cat I want, Huey. And you don't really do anything like that. Do you. Huey?

(Pause.)

Huey, if you are shitting on something, I will kill you.

(Pause.)

I have a pretty red dress. I get my hair done. I take care of myself. I have a voice. I have a body. I can't see any of it. I have nothing to do with them. Sometimes when I'm alone I don't even know if I'm there.

(Pause.)

I think if someone were to touch me, I would know then what I look like. What my shape is. It would prove it. If he were to kiss me, then I would know I have lips. If he whispered in my ear, I would know then that I can hear. If he touched my skin, I would know then. That I am here.

(Pause.)

I clean up after you, and feed you, and you're supposed to love me. That's the agreement. You love me.

(Pause.)

You love me.

8

Dim lights up on THE SALESMAN *and* YOO-HOO GIRL *lying on the couch under a sheet. He's asleep. She sits up, looking out the window, and back at him. Their clothes are scattered on the floor.*

YOO-HOO GIRL

Got dark out.

(Pause.)

You awake?

(She shakes THE SALESMAN. *He grunts and rolls over.)*

I'm gonna tell you something. It's private though so don't go telling everybody you know, ok?

(Pause.)

Sometimes the wind blows through my window and I hear this like whistling on the breeze. Not wind through trees whistling, but, like, lips. It's someone calling for me, I feel. Whistling at my window. Like—uh— like Elvis. Kinda. Like a man in a white shirt and suspenders. He's whistlin' at my window and I look out and he's out there in the shadows in the yard, just out of view but I see him waving his arm for me to come down and join him. He wants me to go with him. I run down the stairs. Quietly. I come out barefoot into the cold wet grass. He takes my hand and we walk and we don't say a word. He's smoking a cigarette and whistlin' smoke through his lips. Like a train. We walk through dirt fields and farms all night, our feet in the soft earth. We come to this huge cliff looking down on the ocean. I've actually never seen the ocean in real life. We're up so high. The sun is just barely starting to creep up making our skins pink. We glow. Now I can just kinda start to see him. The details of his face. In the almost morning light. But we wanna go away, too, before it gets too light. We wanna stay a little in the dark. We look into each other's eyes. His eyes are like tunnels to the center of the world. He kisses me. I feel his whiskers on my chin. Feels good. We put our arms around each other and he puts his lips to my ear. He sings "My Happiness." You know that song? He sings it to me. And then, we just, kind of, *fall.* Backwards off the edge of the cliff we fall and fall and fall still holding onto each other. We hit the water—splash—and keep falling and falling the water getting colder and darker and the pressure building so we get pushed together closer and tighter, he's all up against me in the dark—and finally, gently, we come to rest on the bottom of the ocean. It's soft down there, you know. Little slow motion explosions of soft dirt cloud up around us as we settle. And we're still. Just looking into each other's eyes. And this is how we're gonna be forever. Pushed close and locked together at the bottom of the ocean.

(Pause.)

I was thinking, when I saw you—maybe this is him.

(Pause.)

I don't know why I thought that.

(Pause.)

This isn't really what I'm like, y'know. I'm not usually as girly as this.

THE SALESMAN
(As if in a dream.)

. . . and they lived happily ever—

YOO-HOO GIRL
*(*YOO-HOO GIRL *punches* THE SALESMAN.*)*

Shut up!

THE SALESMAN *grunts.* YOO-HOO GIRL *snuggles up to him.*

Act Two

9

A few weeks later. Lights up on THE SALESMAN *in chair, writing numbers in his notebook.* YOO-HOO GIRL *is on the couch leaning in, watching him.* THE SALESMAN*'s display case is open on the coffee table.*

(Pause.)

YOO-HOO GIRL

Hey.

(Pause.)

Hey!

Pause. She throws a pillow at THE SALESMAN. *He looks up at her.*

YOO-HOO GIRL

What—what else would you want to do? If you weren't a salesman?

THE SALESMAN

Nothing.

YOO-HOO GIRL

You want to do nothing?

THE SALESMAN

No. There's just nothing else I want to do.

(Pause.)

Nothing else I am as good at. It's a curse. I know how to sell.

(Pause. THE SALESMAN *turns back to his accounting.)*

YOO-HOO GIRL

I think you woulda made a good airplane pilot.

THE SALESMAN

Oh yeah?

YOO-HOO GIRL

Um-hm. With the leather hat and the goggles. I'd trust you not to crash me there in the sky.

THE SALESMAN

You're too trusting.

YOO-HOO GIRL

No, I'm not. I don't trust anyone.

(Pause.)

I trust you though.

THE SALESMAN

Why?

YOO-HOO GIRL

Because you're like me. You look used up. I like that. You can't trust new things. Whole things. They let you down. They fail. They reveal their weakness unexpectedly, right when you need them to hold together.

(Pause.)

There's people with little tragedies in their faces. And then there are people who smile too much and mow their lawns too often. Who iron their underwear.

(Laughs.)

Know what I mean?

THE SALESMAN *(Distracted.)*

I do. I think I do. Though I'm sure your habits appear just as strange and senseless to your neighbors.

YOO-HOO GIRL

Probably.—Sometimes I do strange things on purpose, so they'll leave me alone.

THE SALESMAN

You sound like a misanthrope.

YOO-HOO GIRL

A miss who?

THE SALESMAN

Someone who hates other people.

YOO-HOO GIRL

I don't hate them. I love them. I can think what they do is stupid and still love them. Because it is touching. It's strange and sad, the ways people occupy their time. Collecting dolls and stamps. Buying things. Building sheds behind their little houses. They pick out one soap and not another, like it makes some difference, like it says something about them, but in the end the soaps are all the same.

THE SALESMAN

No.

YOO-HOO GIRL

No?

THE SALESMAN

No.

   (Beat.)

My soaps are different.

YOO-HOO GIRL

But—they do the same thing—

THE SALESMAN

No. They're better.

YOO-HOO GIRL

Oh.

   (Pause.)

Why do you sell soap?

THE SALESMAN

Why do I sell soap?

   (Laughs.)

"Why do you sell soap?"—I sell soap because people buy soap. We sell what people will buy. If people were buying third-degree burns I would be out there going door-to-door with a blowtorch.

YOO-HOO GIRL

No!

THE SALESMAN

I sell what people will buy. What they will buy not just once, but over and over. As a product, a bar of soap is nearly perfect. It is perfect because it is consumable and disposable. The customer will always need more.

(Pause.)

The ideal product would be one that evaporates at the same moment that the money changes hands.

YOO-HOO GIRL

Then you'd never have to leave the house.

THE SALESMAN

Hm?

YOO-HOO GIRL

You'd never have to leave. You would just sit here selling to me. Handing me the—the thing that evaporates. And I'd just keep on hand-ing you money. We'd do that all day, then fall asleep and wake up and do it all over again.

(Pause.)

It is perfect.

THE SALESMAN

Until the money runs out.

YOO-HOO GIRL

Or until you run out of that thing you're selling me.

THE SALESMAN

Yes.

(Pause.)

*A sound from the doorway. A newspaper is flung onstage
from off left. They stare at it a moment.*

(Pause.)

YOO-HOO GIRL

Before you came I didn't want anything at all. Not really. You showed
me what I was missing. What I didn't know I needed. And now, I need
it so bad I'm constantly thinking of how I am going to be able to keep
you here with me.

THE SALESMAN

Oh yes?

YOO-HOO GIRL

Mmm-Hmm.

THE SALESMAN

Well.

(Pause.)

You do not need to worry about that.

YOO-HOO GIRL

No?

THE SALESMAN

No.

(Pause.)

I'm not going anywhere.

(Pause.)

10

BATTY, *at home, in a decrepit chair. Her painting stands behind her—nearly finished. She tunes a broken radio, moving between different frequencies of static.*

BATTY

Here it comes, oh yes. Here it comes, HERE it COMES like a metal rain! . . . zzt! Zzzt-zzt! ZZZZZZZZTTTT-AP! An electrical message from the teeth of ANGELS—oh I hear it!—I HEAR it Lord, Angels' metal teeth grinding, shooting sparks, shooting LIGHTNING into me! Mmmmmuh-mmm—

(Epileptic shaking.)

WOAH! Oh!

(Shaking propels her up to standing.)

EVERYTHING FLOWS! Angels blow trumpets of fire in MY HAIR! Angelic FIRE! My brain takes off its hat in divine obedience to the CREATOR OF ELECTRICITY! O ANGEL HORSES chewing haloes of FIRE in their teeth! O Sweet Lord—I mean BUSINESS! I got no BRAINS! I am just a Baby! A newborn BABY remade and washed clean in the showering spark of your attention Lord! I know only six words only SIX words my God, and they are:

(Counting off the words on one upstretched hand.)

O MY SWEET ATOMIC JESUS—LOVE YOUR FUCKING NEIGH-BOR!!! AHHHHHHHHHH!

A rolled up newspaper lands in front of her. She collapses howling in her chair.

11

AMY *alone center stage in chair, talking on an orange rotary phone with her mother. Eyes shut tightly. A pillow clutched in her lap.*

AMY

. . . No—no I haven't. Not yet.—No.—No, but I have—I have been looking.—Well, Mother, it's not as if—it's not as if these things just happen.—I want that, too.—I do.—I do!—No.—No everything is fine. It is going very well. I think I'm going to get a raise. But—yes. But I was thinking—I was thinking that I wanted to get some new shoes.—No, I know it and it—Well, Mother—but perhaps if I had new shoes, something—it might help me—I know you're not.—No.—Ok.—Alright.—I'm sorry.—Huey's fine. Yes, I am looking at him right now.—No, he's no bother.—I will.—No, he loves me.—He does!—I'll kiss him for you.— Ok. I'll see you Sunday.—Ok.—I love you, Mom.—Goodbye.

AMY *hangs up the phone. She sits staring out at the audience for a minute. She looks as if she wants cry.*

(Pause.)

AMY *inhales loudly. Holding her breath, she stands, goes out of her light, turns on a radio. The song "Among My Souvenirs" sung by Connie Francis as* AMY *returns to her light wearing a formal gown over her clothes. She smiles and silently greets the imagined people at this party. She stops in her light. She begins improvising a slow, strange dance with her eyes closed, her arms out. She loses herself in it. Exhales loudly.*

A newspaper thrown from offstage lands at her feet. She stops. Stares at the newspaper. AMY *slowly turns her back to the audience. Music fades, slow BLACKOUT as* AMY *turns away.*

12

The next day. Dim lights. THE SALESMAN *is sitting, eyes closed, stage right. There is a knock at the door.* THE SALESMAN*'s eyes open. Lights up slowly. Another knock.* THE SALESMAN *looks at the door. Another knock.* THE SALESMAN *stands, and goes to the door.*

THE SALESMAN

Yes goddamit I'm coming—

(Another knock.)

YES! I said.

He opens the door: THE PAPERBOY *stands in the doorway with his sack. They stare at each other.*

THE PAPERBOY

—Hi,—

THE SALESMAN

"Hi."

THE PAPERBOY

Uh, is—

THE SALESMAN

Can I help you?

THE PAPERBOY

Can I see—

THE SALESMAN

What are you looking for?

THE PAPERBOY

I'm the paperboy.

THE SALESMAN

I can see you're the paperboy. Would you like to come in?

(Pause.)

THE PAPERBOY

Is the girl who's usually here—is she here?

THE SALESMAN

Come inside.

(Pause.)

Come on, you don't have to be shy. We're all friends here.

(THE PAPERBOY *enters.*)

Take a seat, son.

(THE PAPERBOY *heads towards the chair stage right.*)

Uh-uh.

(Beat, then pointing.)

On the couch there.

THE PAPERBOY *sits on the couch.*

THE PAPERBOY

I can't really stay very long—it's Thursday. I'm collecting today. I mean that's why I knocked otherwise I wouldn't—on Thursdays I collect. We all do. On Thursdays.

(Pause.)

It's ninety-five cents.

(Pause.)

THE SALESMAN

Hey, hey! Slow *down* there, little man! How'd we get to *money* so quick, huh? Does *everything* have to boil down to the *bottom* line all the time? Huh? Look look look: Here we are, it's a *beautiful* afternoon, the sun is *shining* outside the window, I am *new* to the neighborhood, you are a local youth . . . let's just sit here and—get to know each other.

Right? Like *people*. like people used to do. Forget your *job* two min-
utes and —can't you? Honestly, it's, it's—how old are you?

THE PAPERBOY

Sixteen.

THE SALESMAN

Sixteen and running around like a goddamn—*banker*, like a— "Where's
my money? I have to get going! Baw baw baw!" Jesus, you'll give yourself a heart attack before you're seventeen, you know that? Like a . . .
Lookit: Let's just *relax* and enjoy the pleasure of each other's company
for a breath. Can we do that?

THE PAPERBOY

Ok.

THE SALESMAN

Ok?

    (Beat.)

THE PAPERBOY

Ok.

THE SALESMAN

Ok then! Ok *ok*! You want a soda?

THE PAPERBOY

I don't know—

THE SALESMAN

We have Grape and we have Cherry and we have Cream.

THE PAPERBOY

    (Pause.)

Cherry. Please.

THE SALESMAN

Cherry! Excellent. Sit tight. I will be right back.

    THE SALESMAN *exits.* THE PAPERBOY *waits nervously.* THE
    PAPERBOY *reaches out to pick the doll-shaped music box
    on the table.* THE SALESMAN *returns with a bottle of Grape
    soda.* THE PAPERBOY *pulls his arm back quickly.*

THE SALESMAN

Only had grape. Hope that's okay.

> (*Beat.* THE SALESMAN *pulls a bottle opener out of his pocket and opens the bottle with a flourish.*)

There you are, sir—

> (THE PAPERBOY *takes the bottle, sniffs. Beat.*)

Don't worry, son, I didn't piss in it! Ha!

> (THE PAPERBOY *hesitates, then takes a very small sip.*)

So. How long have you been delivering the papers?

THE PAPERBOY

I don't know—

THE SALESMAN

Approximately. Take a guess.

THE PAPERBOY

Three years. I guess. Seventh grade.

THE SALESMAN

Since Seventh Grade. Well. That's impressive. When I was sixteen, I couldn't have held—pshhew!—I couldn't have held a job for two days! Couldn't keep my mind off the, uh, siren song of the fair sex, if you know what I mean. I did not have your *drive*. Couldn't manage more than one idea at a time, and more often than not, that idea was bird-dogging cheerleaders and sneaking shots from my daddy's liquor cabinet. I was not like you. No. You: You're smart.

> (*Pause.*)

You like girls though dontcha?

THE PAPERBOY

Sure.

THE SALESMAN

Not just *like* 'em I mean, but—you have *feelings* about them. Thoughts and . . .

(Gestures.)

You follow?

THE PAPERBOY

I think I understand what you're saying—

THE SALESMAN

This isn't about *thinking*, son! It's about *cogitation*, you know? It's *primal*, what I'm talking about. It's about your heart and your—guts and your—whole body just—whoosh! Pow! A tidal wave!—Girl walks by in a yellow dress—whoosh! You are GONE!—Washed Away! That *pit* opens up inside you like a, like a, like an *endless* thirst in the bottom of your stomach!—You know that feeling?

THE PAPERBOY

I think—

THE SALESMAN

Don't tell me "think," son, do you know that feeling?

THE PAPERBOY *(Smiles.)*

—Yeah.

THE SALESMAN

Yeah? Yeah? Yeah I *think* you do! Yeah yeah yeah, I can see it all over you! Like a dog in heat! Am I right? 'S how I was. Exactly how I was. You're not a bad lookin' kid either. Probably fighting them off with a stick. You could take your *pick* of the girls around here, I betcha.

THE PAPERBOY

I don't know.

THE SALESMAN

What's the matter? You don't know.—Wait. Haven't you got a girl?

THE PAPERBOY

No.

THE SALESMAN

Wait a minute. You're telling me a good-looking, hard-working, intelligent young man like yourself has not yet found himself a girl? I am astonished. I am taken aback. I am aghast.

THE PAPERBOY

It's true.

THE SALESMAN

You know, that's a shame. That is *criminal*. In my opinion. I look at you, I can see you've been through some times, good and bad, even at your tender age. I can see that. You're like a treasure waiting to be unlocked. That's what you are. I mean sure, right now, what are you. You're shy, you stutter, you trip over yourself, dress like shit, can't say the right things, kids laugh at you, humiliation around every corner . . . sure. I see it. But inside you? Inside? There's something golden locked up.

(*Beat.*)

Isn't that right?

(*Pause.*)

THE PAPERBOY

. . . Yes.

THE SALESMAN

Oh yes?

THE PAPERBOY

Yes.

THE SALESMAN

Yes. That's right.

(*Pause.*)

And do you know what the key to that lock is? Do you know what's gonna open you up and reveal to the world the man you know you are? The man you know yourself to be? Do you know what—

THE PAPERBOY

I think I know.

THE SALESMAN

—do you *know* the—You do?

THE PAPERBOY

I think so.

THE SALESMAN

Well—Tell it to me then.

THE PAPERBOY

I'm embarrassed to say it.

THE SALESMAN

Aw come on now! After what we're sharing here? After what we've shared?—Ah—now, listen to me: listen. In *all* the places I've been in this world, and *all* the things I've seen, I've learned *one* thing for sure. One true—*rule* to live by.

(*Beat.*)

"Do. Not. Judge." You see? I do not judge.

(*Beat.*)

So tell me.

(*Beat.*)

Tell me.

(*Beat.*)

Tell me.

(*Pause.*)

THE PAPERBOY

I think it's—A girl.

THE SALESMAN

A girl?

THE PAPERBOY

I think so.

THE SALESMAN

Mm Hm. Mm hm. I knew it. You see? We do think alike. So tell me. Who is she? What's she like? This *girl*. Describe her to me.

THE PAPERBOY

She's . . . she's quiet. And. Pretty. Kinda weird. I think a lot of people think she's crazy.—She doesn't know yet. I haven't told her. We barely talk. We can sit together and not talk for hours. We have done. I don't wanna tell her. I don't wanna ruin it. I like to sit and not say anything with her.

(Pause.)

I used to watch her, from out there. Before I knew her. I would watch her dance around her house. She looked like a crazy person. First, I would sit in a tree across the street and watch her. Then I moved into the bushes by the window. Finally I knocked on her door. I brought her a newspaper. So she asked me in, and I came in. I looked around and it was familiar. It was like home, when you think about it or draw it, when you're little.

(Pause.)

THE SALESMAN

Good.

*(*THE SALESMAN *stands, reaches out and grabs* THE PAPER-BOY. *He pulls him close.)*

Good. Good. so. You watch her. You sit with her. You come here. You sit next to her. You shake like a leaf. Your hands shake. Your mouth gets dry. Your leg almost touches hers. You get hard. It's unbearable. Is that right? You make up excuses to come here, to stay longer. You make excuses to get closer to her. Good.

(Pause.)

Now.

(Pause.)

If you come here again, I will cut you open. I will cut you open from the top of your throat to your belly. Your blood, your bones—it will fall out of you like insects and filth. I will cut you open, if you come back here.

(Pause.)

You are a monster. You understand that? You are a disease. I will take your eyes out. If you come back here—

*(*YOO-HOO GIRL *enters.)*

YOO-HOO GIRL

What are you doing? Don't do that!

THE SALESMAN

It's ok.

YOO-HOO GIRL

Let go of him!

THE SALESMAN

No. Look—it's nothing. See?

YOO-HOO GIRL

What are you—

THE SALESMAN

We're getting to know each other. That's all.

YOO-HOO GIRL

What are you doing?

(THE PAPERBOY *runs out. Pause.*)

THE SALESMAN

He's alright. Nothing happened. I didn't do anything to him. We were just talking.

(*Beat.*)

I was teaching him.

YOO-HOO GIRL

Teaching him?

THE SALESMAN

That's all.

(*Pause.*)

YOO-HOO GIRL

But you hurt him. He was scared. I saw him. He ran away.

THE SALESMAN

Well. It's hard sometimes. To learn things.

(*Beat.*)

Some things we need to learn hurt.

(*Pause.*)

13

YOO-HOO GIRL and AMY *are out on the porch down stage center.* YOO-HOO GIRL *sits,* AMY *stands.* AMY *is wearing her tutu and a tiara. Warm late afternoon light.*

AMY

Look at me! Hey! Look—

(AMY *spins around.*)

Don't I—don't I look good?

YOO-HOO GIRL

Yes.

AMY

Do you think I look good or very good?

YOO-HOO GIRL

Very good.

AMY

Am I pretty?

YOO-HOO GIRL

Yes. You are pretty. You are very pretty. I like your smile.

AMY

Really? You're not just saying that?

YOO-HOO GIRL

No. I always thought you were pretty.

AMY

Always.

(*Pause.*)

Did you see me yesterday? I was walking around the street and I'm dancing, and I'm singing. I see all these people turn off their lights. It was night time. It was late at night. I am in the middle of the road. I am surrounded by an audience but they don't want me to know that they can see me—they turn off their lights to hide from me, because they think if I know they are watching, I will stop. They pretend they aren't looking. But I know. But I didn't know if maybe *you* were watching. You didn't see me dancing? A lot of people don't think I can dance. I can dance. I can dance.

(Pause.)

I like you.

YOO-HOO GIRL

I like you, too.

AMY

I find you interesting. People think that I'm interesting because I talk a lot. I move my hands a lot. I can dance. But you're interesting and you don't even have to do anything.

(Pause.)

I kind of hate you because of that. Actually. Just a little.

(Pause.)

Actually, if you weren't so quiet I might think you were more like me. Sometimes I think you're quiet because you think you're better than I am. Is that right?

YOO-HOO GIRL

No. I am quiet because I don't have anything I want to say.

AMY

How come you never do anything?

YOO-HOO GIRL

I am doing something. I am watching you.

AMY

Maybe. But maybe you are looking down at me. Or through me, maybe. I guess that's probably why I hate you.

(Pause.)

It's not hate. It's just—Just a little.

(Pause.)

Mostly though I think you're interesting! What was your favorite part of my dance? I can't really remember 'cause I kinda do it really—I improuh—improv—ah—I do it all spontaneously. I don't think about it or anything. And it kind of gets lost—so—What was your favorite part of my dance?

YOO-HOO GIRL

When you were turning around.

AMY

What time?

YOO-HOO GIRL

With your hands up. Over your head.

AMY

I remember that. Yeah. Hmm.

(Beat, then excited by her new idea.)

You wanna dance with me some time? Me and you? The Shy Girl and The Loud Girl, dancing, in the middle of the street. I've got a coat that you can wear, it's pink, with fringe at the bottom. Mine's yellow, and pink and yellow look great! Stand up for a minute! Stand up! I wanna show you a move!

YOO-HOO GIRL

I can't right now.

AMY

Ok but—But you're gonna do it after, right? You're not gonna leave me hangin' right? You're not gonna abandon me here, huh? 'Cause that happened to me once. Alright?

(AMY improvises a short, expressive dance.)

Sometimes I like to do things that don't really make sense but they're interesting to watch. Like that. You like it?

YOO-HOO GIRL

Yes.

AMY

It's kind of fun right? I started when once I got really mad at my mom, she caught me in my room doing some stuff.

(Pause.)

What's the matter with you?

(Pause.)

YOO-HOO GIRL

He's different. He's changed.

(Pause.)

He used to smile, to kiss me and smell my hair. Now he looks at me and I can see I am repulsive to him. He doesn't go out anymore. He doesn't work. He just sits in his chair with his eyes closed. When he opens his eyes and looks at me, he is disgusted.

(Pause.)

He—he isn't sexual with me anymore. He says he can't. He says it doesn't work. Not with me. Sometimes it does but then it's angry and without tenderness. Without any love in it.

(Pause.)

I think there used to be love in it. But maybe that was a mistake. There was love in it before, I think.

(Pause.)

I want him to leave but I am afraid. I am afraid he will be all alone without me.—No. He won't hurt me. I could hurt him though.—And—I am afraid sometimes that there won't be another. That as ugly as he is, that he is the man, that he was the man in my dreams.

(Pause.)

What if he is?

(Pause.)

Do you think?

(Pause.)

He's vicious. Like an animal. "I'm a wolf and you're a rabbit. I am going to eat you." Because—

(Pause.)

There's no reason. It's just this way.

(Pause.)

Where does it come from? Do you know?

(Pause.)

AMY

. . . did you see me dancing yesterday? I was out in the street. I just made it up as I went along. Did—did you like it? Was it good?

AMY *sings quietly to herself and dances.*

14

THE SALESMAN *sits in a chair, eyes closed.* YOO-HOO GIRL
enters.

YOO-HOO GIRL
(Softly.)

Hey. Hey. Are you listening to me? I will speak quietly and slowly. So
we do not misunderstand each other.—Are you listening?

(Pause.)

I think I have to ask you to leave. I'm sorry. You know—things are—

(Pause.)

Don't yell. Please. I want to say it to you so you understand. So it
doesn't hurt. I know it seems mean—

(Pause.)

Please—you have to—

(Breaking down.)

Leave! Just leave! Leave!

YOO-HOO GIRL *falls, head on the floor. Long pause.* THE
SALESMAN *stands, walks over to her. Kneels. Puts her head
on his lap.*

YOO-HOO GIRL

. . . please. You have to. You have to . . .

(Pause.)

THE SALESMAN *(He strokes her hair.)*

The idea, the goal towards which we struggle, is freedom from material
want. That is, we struggle to stop struggling. After a certain number of

years. You rise to a point where the work you have already done continues to *produce*, to produce for you, without effort, effortlessly. There are people below you, whose labor you profit from. You have risen above it and then you're free.

>   *(Pause.)*

But. Not yet. Always not yet. Until the end. Until you're too old to move. All you can do is sit and remember all the fucking time you wasted. To get here.

>   *(Pause.)*

I say this because I'm tired. I don't want to sell things anymore. I don't want to work. I don't want to do anything. I am tired. I don't want to wake up tomorrow. I am tired. I've done it already. Won't the days stay done? But no.

>   *(Pause.)*

So. I am someone's nightmare. You will shake your head and deny it, try to console me. I don't need consolation. It is not a burden. It's not a wound. It's a pleasure, actually. To be what you know you are. To be, for example, a monster. But even now, even when you want me to vanish, even when you want me to never have been here at all—you will deny it.

>   *(Pause.)*

I wish I could sing the way you picture it. Whisper in your ear. Read to you as you fall asleep with your head on my lap. Watch you breathe there. Kiss you as you snore. Be the dream you are dreaming. We have a house, a cat. Like a drawing in crayon, black curls of smoke from the chimney. A child's drawing. That's how you must see it. I imagine. Inside your head.

>   *(Pause.)*

You are the girl at the end of the road.

>   *(Pause.)*

I will take whatever I need from you. Because if I do not take it I will not get it at all. I am not your guest. Asking me politely to pack my bags and go—No. I am staying. I will stay. If you yell, I will go deaf. I will go blind. Burn the house down. I don't care. I am not your other half. You see? You have no other half. Half is all there is. You see? So.—so.—so.

(Pause.)

It's very quiet up here tonight . . .

15

Fade music as lights come to full. AMY *out on the street in front of her house looking frantically for her cat.* BATTY *is walking by.*

AMY

Huey? Huey? Aw, come on! HUEY!—Meow! Meow! Meow!

BATTY

Hey! Hey you! Why don't you shut up and get away from my house!

AMY

What?

BATTY

You! Yes you bigmouth—get out of here! Everyday, every single day you people come and yell your heads off right outside my window! Why can't you just be quiet? Aw, you shits! You make my head hurt! You want to make my head hurt! You're trying to kill me!

(Starts weeping a bit.)

You shits . . .

AMY *(Ignoring* BATTY.*)*

Huey? HUEY!

BATTY *(Imitating* AMY.*)*

"Huey! Huey! Huey!"

AMY

Hue-ey!

BATTY

"Huey! Huey! Oink oink oink!"

AMY

Stop it! What are you doing? Why are you doing that? Why are you so mean? My cat is missing! My cat! Do you understand?

BATTY

"Huey! Oink! Huey! Oink! Huey!"

AMY

Shut UP!

BATTY

"Huey! Huey! Huey!"

AMY

Shut up! Shut up! Aw—

(AMY *begins to cry, sits, face in hands.*)

You're going to confuse him! He's just a baby. He's a kitten. I came home from work and I never see him he just sits under the couch all the time stupid fucking cat and he just ran out the door—oh he's so fucking stupid he ran right from the couch out the door! He's a kitten— he doesn't know where he is. He doesn't know how to get back. He's gonna be scared and it's getting dark and he's gonna starve to death or get attacked by a dog—he's so stupid—

(AMY *cries.*)

BATTY

Aw no! Aw no!

(*Pause.*)

No.

AMY

He's my little heart . . . he—he never lets me touch him . . .

Pause. BATTY *walks over to* AMY. *She steps behind her. Reaches out one hand and pats her on the head.*

BATTY

Sure. Sure. Sure.

(*Pause.*)

Hey—uh—are you a little boy? Or a girl?

AMY

What?

BATTY

Are you a pretty little boy? Or a girl?

(BATTY *sniffs* AMY.)

Mmmm.

AMY

I'm—I'm a girl.

BATTY

(Jubilant.)

Oooh-hoo! I knew it I knew it I KNEW it! You look just like a pretty little girl! You got pretty hands. I like your braids, pretty little girl.

AMY

. . . Thanks.

BATTY

Yes I do. Heh. I like you. You are pretty. Look at those teeth!

AMY

I had braces.

BATTY

What a smile. Hey! Don't you know that the nuclear war is starting up now, don't you? Any minute now! The bombs are gonna come flying out of the sky BOOOM!!! Burning everything in sight! There's gonna be nothing left!

AMY

I—I guess I didn't know that.

BATTY

Oh, yeah. Except me! Heh! I planned ahead. I'm goin' down to my basement, gonna lock the door 'til things calm down a little. Y'know—

A pretty girl like you'll get eaten right up in nuclear war! Nuclear war LOVES pretty girls like you! They're the first to go!

(Pause. Looks at AMY.*)*

I'd hate to see you get burned up in nuclear war, It's such a waste of—skin—

*(*BATTY *touches* AMY*'s face. Pause.)*

Eh—you wanna come down to my basement with me and look at the catalogues 'til the bombs stop dropping? Nuclear war is boring—it makes me so tired—it wouldn't be so bad to have a pretty girl down there with me.

AMY

I don't think I can do that—

BATTY

Please? I have to go down to the basement, that's the only safe place but—I'll tell ya—hey this is a secret don't go blabbing it around: I'm afraid of the dark.

*(*BATTY *giggles.)*

It's true! Come on pretty girl. Just come sit with me a little bit. You can help me open my mail. Ok? Maybe you can entertain me, you know the radio melts down in nuclear war . . . you know that don't you? What can you do—you can—you can—what can you do?

AMY

I can—I—dance . . .

BATTY

Oh! Oh! Oh yes! Oh that's very good! Oh my! Oh you can dance and I will watch you! And after we can drink iced tea and put on fancy clothes and—just—be—quiet . . . Oh yes! Mmm!

> BATTY *pulls* AMY *to her feet and begins singing "The Teddy Bears' Picnic" as she leads* AMY *off.* AMY *allows herself to be led. They exit.*

16

THE SALESMAN *is dimly lit, sitting in his chair downstage right. His eyes are closed; he is sleeping. Middle of the night.*

YOO-HOO GIRL *is standing barefoot on her porch. She inhales deeply. Looking at neighbors houses, listening to peepers and crickets and frogs. A sudden rustling is heard offstage left.* YOO-HOO GIRL *turns, startled. Looks out left.*

YOO-HOO GIRL

Hey!

(Pause. Another rustle is heard.)

Hey! Is somebody in my bushes?

(Pause.)

Hey, man, I can see your sneakers.

(Rustle. Pause.)

Come out of there you!

YOO-HOO GIRL *exits.*

YOO-HOO GIRL (O.S.)

C'mere!

YOO-HOO GIRL *re-enters with* THE PAPERBOY *in tow. A couple of leaves are stuck in his hair.*

YOO-HOO GIRL

What the hell are you doing fooling around in my bushes in the middle of the night?

*(*THE PAPERBOY *doesn't answer.)*

Huh? You better tell me. I don't want to but I will call your mother. You think she's gonna be happy to find out her son's been out playing in other people's foliage at two in the morning?

THE PAPERBOY

I was looking for something. Something I lost.

YOO-HOO GIRL

What could you have possibly lost in my bushes?

THE PAPERBOY

A pocket knife. I think I dropped it on my route. I was throwing the papers, y'know, on to people's porches and I think my knife somehow slipped out of um my pocket and I think I must've thrown it. Over there.

Pause. They look at each other.

YOO-HOO GIRL

You lost your knife, huh?

THE PAPERBOY

Yeah.

YOO-HOO GIRL

Did you find it?

THE PAPERBOY

Uh, no.

YOO-HOO GIRL

Well. You wanna sit down a minute?

THE PAPERBOY

Ok.

They sit. Pause.

YOO-HOO GIRL

Beautiful night.

THE PAPERBOY

Yeah.

YOO-HOO GIRL

(Reaching to pick up her fudge.)

Hey, I got a piece of fudge I just made this afternoon. You wanna share it with me?

THE PAPERBOY

Sure.

YOO-HOO GIRL

Ok. I'll split it with you. You got a knife?

THE PAPERBOY *(Reaching in his pocket.)*

Yeah, I got—Oh.

(They look at each other for a moment.)

I was watching.

YOO-HOO GIRL

Watching what?

THE PAPERBOY

That guy in there. I was watching him sleep.

YOO-HOO GIRL

You were?

THE PAPERBOY

Yeah.

YOO-HOO GIRL

How come?

THE PAPERBOY

I don't know.

YOO-HOO GIRL

What did you want to see?

THE PAPERBOY

Nothing.—I just wanted to see him while he was sleeping is all.—I like
to watch people when they don't know I'm there.

(Pause.)

That sounds kind of weird, doesn't it?

YOO-HOO GIRL

Yeah.

THE PAPERBOY

I guess it is. I like to do it though.

> YOO-HOO GIRL *cuts the fudge in half and gives* THE PAPER-
> BOY *a piece.*

YOO-HOO GIRL

Well—have some fudge.

THE PAPERBOY

Thanks.

> *(They eat fudge.)*

YOO-HOO GIRL

Why don't you stop by anymore?

THE PAPERBOY

I've been busy. With the papers.

YOO-HOO GIRL

Are there more papers now then there used to be?

THE PAPERBOY

Some.

> *(Pause.)*

YOO-HOO GIRL

I don't believe you.

> *(Pause.)*

THE PAPERBOY

I—I don't think I like your boyfriend. Very much.

YOO-HOO GIRL

You don't?

THE PAPERBOY

Yeah.

YOO-HOO GIRL

Oh. So that's why you don't come?

THE PAPERBOY

Yeah.

YOO-HOO GIRL

Is that the only reason?

THE PAPERBOY

Yeah.—What else would it be?

(Pause.)

YOO-HOO GIRL

Do you ever watch me?

THE PAPERBOY

I watch a lot of people. It's just something I do.

YOO-HOO GIRL

So, you do watch me.

THE PAPERBOY

—Sometimes.

YOO-HOO GIRL

"Sometimes."—You watch me a lot?

THE PAPERBOY

As much as anybody else. I guess.

YOO-HOO GIRL

Oh.

(Pause.)

For a long time?

THE PAPERBOY

Maybe a year.

YOO-HOO GIRL

This isn't dirty for you is it?

THE PAPERBOY

What? Oh! No! No! Not like that! No! It's just—

(Pause.)

It's like being invisible. Seeing the world without yourself in it. You get closer to 'em, to people, that way. I read their mail, y'know. The mail of normal people. Their grocery lists. I see what kind of soup they eat. All these details that make up their lives. It is gross, do you think? But it's so pretty. The choices they made. The details of their lives are so beautiful, so normal, and you can never see them with people in the way. They won't let you. People are ashamed. They cover it up, like it's dirty. The things they do in private. Sometimes I imagine that I am the last person on Earth. I wake up one day and—like a bomb went off and everyone just evaporated but their houses stay the same. All the traces and scraps intact. With them all gone and out of the way, I could see it all. I would know so much about people. I would—I would be so close to them then. Like a museum but about now instead of cavemen or Indians. Like in a doll house. Like a museum.

                    YOO-HOO GIRL

Hm.

        (Pause.)

                    THE PAPERBOY

But—I guess I do maybe look more at your house. More than any other.

                    YOO-HOO GIRL

Hm. Am I more normal than other people?

                    THE PAPERBOY

No!

        (Laughs.)

No, that's for sure!

                    YOO-HOO GIRL

So how come?

                    THE PAPERBOY

Because—you know why?

                    YOO-HOO GIRL

Because why?

                    THE PAPERBOY

Because—You're my favorite person, y'know. 'Cause you're like me, I think. It's different outside. At school. Out there they'll hit you. They'll hit you because your bicycle cost more money than theirs. Or because it cost less. They'll hit you for no reason at all. The hitting isn't so bad as that they want to. Why do they want to? To me? They wouldn't hit you. You're a girl. If I was a girl, they would still hit me. They can smell me, I decided. Smell something different on me. Something they hate about me I didn't choose. When I was little, like four, every fight got settled by an adult. The blocks get taken away. We cry, it isn't fair, but there's an order. A law we all agree to obey. When I turned eleven I had a birthday party. Me and some friends sat out on the steps of my house. We were busting soda cans on the street. Shaking up the cans and throwing them to the ground to make 'em burst and spray. It looked cool, like a volcano. We were laughing. We did it 'til all the soda was gone. I walk out into the street. I was gonna clean it up, I was. All of a sudden, this giant neighbor, this bald guy with a red beard, fucking huge, walks out of his house. He is heading towards me. I stand still. He says, "Hey," and waves me over. I go there and when I get close he grabs me, grabs my arm, his face is red, his teeth are stained, his hand and face are huge. He says, "I've been watching you. You make me sick. Don't you know? Someone had to make those cans? They cost money. Someone has to clean it up. Don't look for your friends. It's just you and me here. Why don't you clean up your own fucking mess?" He shakes me once. This guy across the street who never said anything to me before. I am standing in the middle of the street shaking and starting to sort of cry cause I'm so scared and these stupid soda cans are rolling around at my feet. That's when I figured it out. That order? It's a lie. The world we grew up in in no way prepares us for the world we come to inhabit. That's why I watch you. That's why I hang around. Because your house is safe. Because I feel sure you don't hate me. Because you smell like me.

> *They stare at each other.*
>
> YOO-HOO GIRL *and* THE PAPERBOY *slowly kiss. They stay like that a moment.* THE SALESMAN *enters.*

THE SALESMAN

What—what are you doing?

> *(Pause.)*

What is this?

(Pause.)

No. No. No. No. You are not doing this. No.

> THE PAPERBOY *tries to back away.* THE SALESMAN *grabs* THE PAPERBOY *by the wrist and drags him back inside the house.* YOO-HOO GIRL *follows.*

THE SALESMAN

No. No. What are you doing?—

YOO-HOO GIRL

It was a game—we were playing—

THE SALESMAN

You were playing? You were playing? No. No. You repulse me. What did you think? You don't think. You have no mind. You are just a body. You are disgusting. You are a body with no bones. You are a body full of diseased mouths. You just want. You have no mind. You can only think with your skins. With your guts. You sicken me.

> *(To* THE PAPERBOY*.)*

You. Come here. Boy. Come here!

> *(Takes* THE PAPERBOY *and pulls him close, holding him so they are both facing* YOO-HOO GIRL*.)*

Yes. So. Were you playing? What were you doing? Is this what you wanted. Isn't it? This is what it is all about. Isn't it. You talk and look— you—you come here, and you—you bring gifts—you feel well around her? No. It's this. This. You—what? You "love" her? And what is that? This. You're "courting"? "Your eyes my love like stars in the night sky—" —No. You see? It is this. You fuck. You fuck. See? This hand like this—It is this, this, this—it is your hand here, and I hear you breathing—

YOO-HOO GIRL

Stop it! Stop it.

THE SALESMAN

Your breath is warmer now—

YOO-HOO GIRL

Stop it. Please.

THE SALESMAN

Why? What am I doing? Am I breaking something? No. What am I doing?

YOO-HOO GIRL

What are you doing? What are you doing!

> YOO-HOO GIRL *leaps on* THE SALESMAN. *They fall together. She is on top of him, he lies on the ground.*

THE SALESMAN

Get off me!

YOO-HOO GIRL

No! No! What's wrong with you? Why do you do this? Look at me! Do you see?

> (YOO-HOO GIRL *grabs* THE SALESMAN *by his hair and pulls his face close to hers.)*

I am very angry. Do you understand? You have upset me. Can you see? I am very angry! Tell me why! Why am I angry?

THE SALESMAN

You're crazy!

> *(She slaps him.)*

YOO-HOO GIRL

No! Tell me why!

THE SALESMAN

No! You're crazy! Get off me! What are you doing?

> *(She slaps him.)*

YOO-HOO GIRL

Tell me! Why am I angry? Why do you think I am angry?

> *(She pulls his hair. He yells.)*

I need to hear you. You understand? Say the words! Why!

THE SALESMAN

What do you want? I don't know! You're crazy! I don't know what you want!

(She slaps him.)

YOO-HOO GIRL

Why am I angry?

THE PAPERBOY

What are you doing?

YOO-HOO GIRL

I'm teaching him. I'm teaching. He has to learn.

THE SALESMAN *yells and throws* YOO-HOO GIRL *off of him.*

THE SALESMAN

Get off me! Get off me! Get off!

She falls backwards against the coffee table. She goes still.

There is a long pause.

THE SALESMAN *stands.* THE PAPERBOY *remains in the corner. They stare at her and at each other. After a long moment* THE SALESMAN *exits stage right. He returns with his sample case, his jacket and a small suitcase.*

THE SALESMAN

Well. So. And.—Be a good boy. Hey. Look at me. Be good. Hm? It only hurts for a while. And all that.

THE SALESMAN *exits. The lights return to the look of The Prologue. "My Happiness," sung by Elvis, fades up.*

BLACKOUT.

THE END